The 6-Step Guide to 6 Figure Blogging

Table of Contents

Introduction

You have undoubtedly heard of the viability of niche blogging. Not only are blogs easier to build and optimize for the search engines, but they are also incredible "viral tools" used to penetrate even the most competitive niche markets.

Popular bloggers Darren Rouse and celebrity gossip blogger, Perez Hilton are generating 7-figures a year just by posting fresh, interesting and relevant content to their popular, ever-growing blog sites, but let's make one thing clear – profitable blogging isn't just for seasoned writers or media stars.

Even a brand new blogger can begin to build a steady income with high quality blogs in countless niche markets!

And here's why: Blogs are very different than traditional websites. Rather than static pages, they are full-featured *"communities"* that attract repeat visitors who interact and communicate with each other.

In other words, blogs offer a **"sticky"** element that is rarely found with traditional, static websites, plus, since blogs are incredibly easy to set up, and maintain, they are also the most popular website format for both seasoned entrepreneurs and newbies alike.

In fact, you can build a fully functional blog in a matter of a few short hours, even if you've never done it before!

So how can you make money with your own quality blog?

For starters, high profit bloggers know the value of high quality, relevant content. They also know how to call on the *'entertainment factor'* to further their brand and ensure that their blog visitors continue to drop by on a regular basis.

If you do this, you'll never struggle to build a community of loyal followers, and through your blogs ever-growing community, you'll be able to maximize your traffic (and income) just from visitors who tell others about your website.

When you give people an opportunity to share their thoughts, provide feedback and connect with each other on a personal level, you'll find it much easier to build a high-active, profitable community with less time and less effort than anything you've ever tried before!

In fact, one of the most attractive elements of a blog is in just how much your visitors can power up your website!

From leaving comments, to pinging, re-publishing your articles, to linking directly to your site, you'll be able to build brand awareness, develop an active community and generate unstoppable targeted traffic in no time at all, just by letting your visitors power up your website for you!

The 6 Figure Blogging Report offers a comprehensive start-up guide so that you can begin building your very own high profit blog quickly, and easily.

Let's get started!

STEP 1- Choosing The Right Theme

There are thousands of themes available for WordPress, and it can be very difficult to choose the right one if you're not quite sure what to look for.

Choosing a theme should be based on *profitability and flexibility.*

You need a clean, simple theme that emphasizes your ads, while showcasing your content so that visitors are comfortable navigating through the different areas of your website without getting lost, or finding it difficult to locate the content that is most important to them.

Many free themes focus primarily on the cosmetic value, rather than giving you the flexibility that you need to effectively monetize your blog.

But there's now a solution to our theme-hunting difficulties! ☺

One theme that many of the leading professional bloggers are using is called Socrates.

This theme was developed in partnership with Adsense mastermind, Joel Comm and it was designed to increase CTR on your ads, while automating your ability to monetize your blogs from start to finish.

If you are interested in making money with AdSense, this is a fantastic theme to use. Plus, you can easily integrate additional monetization strategies, including affiliate products through Amazon and ClickBank's marketplace.

All you have to do is enter your AdSense publisher ID and your ClickBank ID and ads will instantly be placed into the theme in the most critical areas for high CTR.

Whichever theme you choose, make sure you choose one that is based on **monetization rather than appearance.**

You can spruce up any theme imaginable, but if it's foundation is difficult to work with, or your visitors feel awkward navigating through your different sections, you'll find it harder to switch over later, so be careful choosing a fully optimized theme that provides you with the flexibility you need to customize it so that it works for your niche market.

STEP 2- Choosing Your Blogs Topic

In order to develop a successful blog, you need to focus on a specific topic.

Every profitable blog needs to be targeted and carry a theme, so that the content is able to cater to a specific segment of your market, without leaving visitors confused or overwhelmed.

Perez Hilton created a successful blog by writing about celebrity gossip. Bloggers like Ana Hoffman and ShoeMoney made their fortunes by writing about Internet Marketing and online business, while Darren Rowse from ProBlogger, teaches people how to build and monetize online blogs.

Each blog has a specific theme, a niche and a focus so that its able to cater specifically to a segment of their market. This is very important! Do not try to create an all-encompassing blog, otherwise you'll lose focus and find it difficult to retain your visitors or to build your own distinct brand.

When just starting out, concentrate on small niche blogs in order to build income and establish your foothold in your niche market (plus, it will give you valuable experience that you can use to later expand into other markets).

Once you have successfully developed a blog focusing on a smaller niche market, you can now venture into new, mainstream markets!

STEP 3- Quick & Easy Keyword Research

To get traffic in the beginning, keyword search is critical.

If you simply create content for your website without optimizing your articles for important and relevant keywords, you'll struggle to generate targeted traffic.

Keywords power your traffic campaigns and ultimately work towards gaining a secure position within the major search engines.

When you are able to rank for relevant keywords, you'll be able to generate organic, natural (and highly targeted) traffic from search engines like Google and Yahoo – absolutely FREE!

Organic traffic is the "cream of the crop" as far as traffic goes, because these visitors are exceptionally targeted.

When evaluating potential keywords, I highly recommend using the Google Keyword Tool available at:
https://adwords.google.com/select/KeywordToolExternal

This tool will help you quickly find high-traffic keywords in your niche, as well as to help you effectively evaluate the level of competition targeting different keywords, so that you can find less competitive, alternative phrases.

You should look for keywords that have at least 1,000 monthly searches, and no more than 150,000 results in Google.

Just enter the keyword string, wrapped "in quotes" into Google and you'll find out how many other websites are using that specific keyword based on the search results.

Every time you create a post, it should be based on one of the keywords you found. Use the keyword in the title of the post, at least twice in the content itself, and in the tags.

Don't forget to include synonyms as well. Recent updates at Google have indicated that synonyms are important to overall ranking, so it's very important that you write as naturally as possible and include various synonyms in your writing.

Why?

Because synonyms help Google determine your overall site theme, based on related keywords found throughout the pages and content on your website.

For example, if you are writing an article about "golf clubs", you might also want to include words like "iron", "wood", "putter", and some of the popular brand names for golf clubs. This will help you rank much better than simply repeating your main keyword over and over.

You will also want to make sure to use these keywords as anchor text whenever you create backlinks to your articles or content pages.

Google places a heavy weight on the anchor text used to link to a page as indication of its overall relevancy, so you will want to make sure at least half of your backlinks include your main keyword with additional backlinks focusing on alternative keywords, so that you're able to rank for many different terms!

STEP 4- Optimizing Your Blog

Optimizing a blog for the major search engines is relatively simple, and it's an important part of your blogs structure because it ultimately makes the difference between a high ranking blog easily found in the search engines, or a blog buried on Page 20!

When you first create your blog, the majority of its traffic will come directly from the search engines. This means that in order to maximize your traffic and overall outreach, you need to fully optimize your entire blog so that it's able to solidify top placement.

The higher your site appears in the search results, the more traffic you'll receive.

One easy way of optimizing your website automatically, is with the powerful SEOPressor utility.

This plugin was created to make SEO ridiculously easy, and it goes much, much further than any free solution can. In fact, you can fully optimize your entire blog in a matter of minutes after uploading and activating this powerful plugin.

Not to mention, you'll save a tremendous amount of time!

STEP 5- Build Brand Awareness

Branding is absolutely essential for bloggers, because it's one of the easiest ways of creating an online presence, while developing a memorable website that people will eagerly return to.

Never forget how effective word-of-mouth marketing can be!

There are two ways to brand yourself:

1. You can brand your blog.
2. You can brand yourself.

If you choose to brand your website itself, you will want to focus on making sure people always remember the name of your blog, followed by your blogs sub title/slogan and theme.

Your website should have a catchy name, a prominent logo, and you should mention the name of your blog often in order to keep pushing your brand, and building up instant recognition!

If you choose to brand yourself, you will instead make sure people know who you are, what your overall goals are, what you're all about and more importantly, what you can offer them.

You can post pictures of yourself, create compelling videos that highlight your brand, register domain names that represent your brand, develop additional community sites including forums, social media accounts and even additional blogs relating to your primary niche!

All of the world's most successful blogs are highly adept at branding. Blogs like TheFrisky.com do a great job of branding blog names, and bloggers like John Chow and Perez Hilton are masters at branding their own names.

Consider the different ways that you can establish a unique brand, all your own. Perhaps you could create a newsletter that helps you establish relationships with your target audience, while developing a brand through quality content releases, regular updates and of course, new content, surveys, polls and events available to those who frequently visit your blog.

Reward your visitors for their loyalty with contests, events and by consistently developing fresh, unique and informative content that directly helps them!

STEP 6- Monetizing Your Blog

There are several different ways to make money with your blog and you'll want to combine a series of monetization strategies into your blog so that you are able to maximize your income.

Let's start with Adsense!

AdSense

With Adsense, you are paid for every click made to advertisements featured throughout your blog. It's free to join as an Adsense advertiser, and you are able to generate code that you simply copy and paste into your blogs pages that will feature advertising boxes from various merchants.

To sign up, visit http://www.Google.com/adsense and create your account. Once you have it all set up, you will be able to customize the size and color scheme of your Adsense advertising boxes so that it blends well with your existing blog's theme.

This is an easy way to start making money with your blog even with little traffic, because rather than selling directly to your target audience, you are simply making money each time they click on your ads, costing them nothing in the process (you earn money even if they never purchase anything from these external websites).

You can also create campaigns within your Adsense account so that you can have a number of different advertisements across a network of blogs, which will give you the ability to determine what advertisements are converting and working well, and which ones may need to be tweaked to better perform.

You will also want to create individual channels for each blog that you plan to feature Adsense on, so that you can determine what campaigns are working well, and track the CTR of each advertisement.

If you find that a particular ad isn't preforming well, you can choose to change the placement, color scheme or size of the ad, as well as the general channel so that your advertisements are highly targeted to your audience.

Just remember to really call attention to those ads by choosing a theme like Socrates.

Side Note: From personal experience, larger square ad boxes convert better, with the colors modified to blend well with your website. You don't want these advertisements to intrude on your visitors experience navigating throughout your website, but instead focus on creating advertisements that fit well within your template and use a similar color scheme.

Start with the 250x250 square ad boxes or the 300x250 medium size if your blog's theme can accommodate it. Otherwise, the tower advertisements can be integrated into the side panels of most blog themes.

The 728x90 leaderboard ad box is great for the upper portion of your blog's theme, right under the header, or at the very bottom, featured within the footer area of your website.

CPA

CPA can be extremely profitable, but it is also tricky. Choosing the right ads is very important, but you have to keep in mind that you must monitor CPA campaigns very closely.

Most CPA campaigns only last a few weeks to a few months, and they can be removed without any notice at all. Because of this, you have to continually watch campaigns and change them when they become inactive so you don't lose money.

Here are a few programs and networks to help you get started:

CPA Lead
http://www.CPALead.com

Hydra Network
http://www.HydraNetwork.com

Advaliant
http://www.Advaliant.com

Never Blue
http://www.NeverBlue.com

Max Bounty
http://www.MaxBounty.com

Affiliate Marketing

There are two major types of products you can promote as an affiliate. You can promote digital products like eBooks and videos, or you can promote physical products like DVD players or computers.

The type of products you will want to promote will depend on your niche. Some niches work equally well with both types of products, but many niches are better suited to one or the other.

For example, the golf niche would work equally well with both physical and digital products. You could just as easily promote an eBook about improving your golf swing as you could a set of golf clubs.

But a niche like "DVD players" is probably better suited to physical products like DVD players, DVD movies, televisions, and surround sound systems.

Paid Advertising

Very successful blogs can charge a lot of money to advertise on them. Some sites charge several thousand dollars per month for advertising, and they may have several advertisers paying this each month!

One great thing about charging for advertising is that you don't have to worry about CTR or sales. You get paid whether the advertiser's ads get clicked or not, and you get paid even if they never make a penny from those ads.

This can be a very significant source of revenue if you have a lot of traffic, but you will need to provide prospective advertisers a lot of information before they will feel comfortable advertising with you.

If you're going to offer paid advertising, you will probably want to install Google Analytics on your blog so you can prove how much traffic you get. You may also want to provide statistics about visitor demographics, as well as average CTR for various spots on your site.

To get started, visit http://www.ClickBank.com and click on the Marketplace link. Then, enter in keywords relating to your market in order to generate a page listing products and services that you can promote as a ClickBank affiliate.

Whenever you view the details of any given offer, you will see stats located under each listing, one of these statistics is called gravity.

The gravity rating in Clickbank.com is just an estimate of the most recent sales for a particular product. The higher the gravity rating, the more popular the product is among affiliates since it appears that the product is receiving a large number of sales.

When a product also has a high gravity rating, since sales are factored in, it means that the product is converting. That's the critical aspect of selecting a product to promote within Clickbank.com. You always want to ensure that the product you are promoting actually converts.

Blog Assignments & Projects

You may occasionally be offered to write posts in exchange for pay. Basically, you will be asked to cover a particular product or website as a news story or review. This can be a good source of revenue, but it requires significantly more work than standard advertising, and usually won't pay as much money.

You will have to research the product, website, or company very thoroughly before you write about it. Don't sacrifice your integrity or your reputation for the sake of money! You need to be certain the company is legitimate and that their offerings are high-quality. You can really ruin your reputation if you recommend something scammy or low-quality.

You will also have to spend time writing the post, and they will expect it to be a thorough and in-depth review if they are paying you.

Just be certain they know you will only write your true opinion, and they will have no say in what you write.

Your reputation will matter a great deal to the success of your blog, so never compromise it for the sake of earning money.

For those who are interested in participating in blog networks that pay you per assignment or project, there are many different opportunities available to even the newest blogger. Here is a break down of the different options available to you:

Pay Per Post

http://www.PayPerPost.com

Pay Per Post is one of the larger services available that offer bloggers the opportunity to get paid for blogging about specific subjects. In fact, they are one of the pioneers of "paid to blog" opportunity-based marketplaces.

Blogitive

http://www.Blogitive.com

This is a super program for start up bloggers as you can earn $5.00 per post regardless of your current traffic, or how new your blog may be. I joined this network immediately after settting up my blog and have experienced great success with it. It's really a lot of fun!

Loud Launch

http://www.LoudLaunch.com

This works similarly to Pay Per Post where you can browse and accept opportunities however it's still growing in size and isn't nearly as popular as Pay Per Post. Still, It's a great opportunity for new blogs and bloggers with very few requirements such as the fact that your blog must be at least two months old and you must have the ability to use Paypal to receive your earnings.

Review Me

http://www.ReviewMe.com

The Review Me program works differently than the Pay Per Post one because with ReviewMe.com, potential advertisers will contact you directly offering to pay you to review their website or blog.

Sponsored Reviews

http://www.SponsoredReviews.com

This site includes aspects of both Pay Per Post and Review Me, in which you can browse and accept offers as well as allow advertisers to contact you directly with project offers.

Blogger Wave

http://www.BloggerWave.com

Blogger Wave can pay you up to $10.00 per post and have very few requirements, making this is a great choice for new bloggers.

Smorty

http://www.Smorty.com

This company will pay you $6.00 + per post with the payments increasing as your blog grows in popularity.

BlogVertise

http://www.BlogVertise.com

Blogvertise works very differently from that of Pay Per Post and Review Me in terms of how opportunities are offered and completed. With Blogvertise, their system matches bloggers to available offers, based on the type of content and ranking.

Link Worth

http://www.LinkWorth.com

LinkWorth is one of the web's largest and most innovative marketing portals that caters to both Advertisers and Partners.